H. U. G. S.
(To live a better life)

(HELPING U GET STRONGER)

Vickie A. Willis

INTRODUCTION

I wanted to do a devotional to walk you through the
art of practicing the Presence of God and living
a life of daily devotion unto the Lord. This
devotional will help to uplift, encourage, empower
and strengthen you in your daily journey. In today's
Journey we face many difficulties; not just because
of the pandemic, but before there was a pandemic
life had a way to deal us intense pressures of
frustrations, quick temperaments, stressful
thoughts, marital and financial challenges, and
physical and fearful challenges. I dare you to say
"BUT GOD!". My objective in writing this
devotional is to let you know that through God's

written and infallible Word, daily personal,
devotional prayer we can learn how to confront and
overcome each situation and come out wiser, better
and stronger. Isaiah 40:29 (KJV) declares, "He
gives us power to the faint; and to them that have no
might he increaseth strength. If you're ready to
travel this new journey together, it requires your
participation. Let's Grow!! Let's Get Stronger!
Let's Go!!!

TABLE OF CONTENTS

,

PART 2

HELPING U
GET
STRONGER!
ISAIAH 40:29

DAY 1

Facing Anxiety

Peace I leave with you, my peace I give unto you: not as the world giveth, give I unto you. Let not your heart be troubled, neither let it be afraid. John 14:27

Beloved, we sometimes believe as long as things are going well that is clarified as peace, but here Jesus was saying it doesn't matter what the case may be if all chaos is around you he has given us a peace on the inside of us right in the mist of all chaos that will not be shaken. The very peace of God. Peace in Hebrew translation is shalom, meaning harmony, wholeness, completeness, prosperity, welfare and tranquility.

Can you remember a time when you experience the shalom (peace) of God in a situation? Write it down below and reflect on it the very next time when you face anxiety...

Father, we thank you that no matter what it looks like or feels like, you have given us a peace that surpasses all.

DAY 2

Facing Anxiety 2

[6] Be careful for nothing; but in every thing by prayer and supplication with thanksgiving let your requests be made known unto God [7] And the peace of God, which passeth all understanding, shall keep your hearts and minds through Christ Jesus. [8] Finally, brethren, whatsoever things are true, whatsoever things are honest, whatsoever things are just, whatsoever things are pure, whatsoever things are lovely, whatsoever things are of good report; if there be any virtue, and if there be any praise, think on these things.

(Philippians 4:6-8)

One of the Greek translations for the word careful is anxious, Paul admonishes us not to be anxious about anything but instead in everything through prayer and supplication with thanksgiving let our request be made known to God and by doing so, watch this beloveds, here comes the promise to the applying of the principle.... the peace of God which passeth, when you see (eth) added to a word it means continues; so, passeth means the peace continues to pass all understanding!! And shall is a

13

command word!! Peace of God Shall continue to
pass all understanding and keep your hearts and
mind through Christ Jesus!!! Not only that
Beloveds, Paul, then tells us what to think on to
maintain that peace; think on whatsoever things are

true, honest, just, pure, lovely, good report, and if there be any virtue and if there be any praise, come on somebody! Think on these things!!

Beloved, after reading today's devotion can you tell me what are the things we should think on to maintain our peace? Write them below!

_____

_____

_____

_____

_____

_____

_____

_____

_____

_____

_____

_____

_____

_____

_____

_____

_____

_____

_____

_____

_____

_____

_____

_____

_____

Prayer: Father, Thank You for Peace that passes all
understanding; In Jesus Name, Amen!

HELPING U
GET
STRONGER!
ISAIAH 40:29

DAY 3

Acceptance

I pray for them: I pray not for the world, but for them which thou hast given me; for they are thine. And all mine are thine, and thine are mine; and I am glorified in them.11 And now I am no more in the world, but these are in the world, and I come to thee. Holy Father, keep through thine own name those whom thou hast given me; that they may be one, as we are. While I was with them in the world, I kept them in thy name: those that thou gavest me I have kept, and none of them is lost, but the son of perdition; that the scripture might be fulfilled. And now come I to thee; and these things I speak in the world, that they might have my joy fulfilled in themselves. I have given them thy word; and the world hath hated them, because they are not of the world, even as I am not of the world.
John 17:9-14

Beloved, Jesus, prayed this prayer in advance for the disciples (us), because he knew we would be rejected for no other reason other than because we are disciples of Christ Jesus. Jesus prays that God, the Father keeps us, protects us, helps us maintain our joy and stay unified with him and each other, because we belong to the Father!! WE ARE ACCEPTED OF THE LORD!

Beloved, what is your take away from today's devotion?

Father, thank you for accepting me even when others
reject me!

Assurance

And Jesus said unto them, Because of your unbelief: for verily
I say unto you, if ye have faith
as a grain of mustard seed, ye shall say unto this mountain,
Remove hence to yonder place; and it
shall remove; and nothing shall be impossible unto you.
Matthew 17:20

Beloved, we can be assured if we trust and believe,
have absolute confidence and reliance in the un-
adulterated word of God, which is having faith, we
can speak to the mountains of poverty, sickness,
disease, murder, racism, , and COVID-19, injustice
and etc; it shall be removed!!! You hear me
beloved!!

There is ABSOLUTLY NOTHING IMPOSSIBLE

TO YOU IF YOU ONLY BELIEVE!

I have a question now beloved, whose report are
you going to believe? Write 3 things you are going
to believe God to do for you by applying this
scripture. Let's go!!

Father, thank you for giving me assurance in your promises through faith in your word!

DAY 5

Courage

Have not I commanded thee? Be strong and of a good courage; be not afraid, neither be thou dismayed: for the Lord thy God is with thee whithersoever thou goest.
Joshua 1:9

Sometimes, we have to be reminded with facing so many cares of the world today that the Lord is with us in the mist of it all!! I just could not imagine Joshua walking with Moses day by day, and all of a sudden he is dead and God says, "okay josh, boy it's your time to lead this tribe to the promise land". Could you imagine that? BUT GOD!! When you have those one on one encounters with the Father and he comes to encourage you and says, be strong and of good courage and don't be afraid, why????
Because I, the Lord am with you, and not just sometimes, not just in some places, whoooweee!! I mean whithersoever we go!!! Come on through Jesus!!! Oh! OK! Ya'll! I Felt my help right there!!

Can you remember a time when you had to remind yourself in your journey that God was with you? Write it ....

_____

_____

_____

_____

_____

_____

_____

_____

_____

_____

_____

_____

_____

_____

_____

_____

_____

_____

_____

_____

_____

_____

_____

_____

_____

_____

_____

_____

Father, we thank you that you have given us courage
to finish the race!!

DAY 6

Facing Cares

Casting all your care upon him; for he careth for you.
1st Peter 5:7

Today Beloved I want to use a personal experience; for many years, I used to feel like it was my responsibility to meet everyone's needs. That is not the plan of God for our lives. It's really a habit of trying to please people. If that's you like it was once me you may want to get delivered from that stronghold. Nonetheless, this is not a deliverance service (smile.) I had a habit of saying yes, when in my heart I really want to say no. I was going when I didn't want to go, giving when I didn't want to give, or have it to give. I was smiling while crying on the inside. There was no real joy. Yes, everybody around me was happy and I was sad and heavy. I had to learn that it was not my responsibility to supply people's needs. If people were going to like me they were going to like me for me and not for what I had to give or not give them. Upon accepting those truths, I was able to be free from the false responsibility of supplying the needs of people and people pleasing and learn that I had to cast my own cares upon the Lord because they were to heavy for me to carry. Just think and there I was trying to carry the burden of others and mine as well. Jesus, thank you!

Beloved, will you cast your cares upon the Lord
today?

_____

_____

_____

_____

_____

_____

_____

_____

_____

_____

_____

_____

_____

_____

_____

_____

_____

_____

_____

_____

_____

_____

Father, thank you for caring for me when I couldn't
care for myself!

DAY 7

Facing Debt

Give, and it shall be given unto you; good measure, pressed
down, and shaken together, and running over, shall men give
into your bosom. For with the same measure that ye mete
withal it shall be measured to you again.
Luke 6:38

All through the Bible we see the principle of
breaking debt is giving, even when it comes down
to the redemption, Jesus gave his life so we can
have an opportunity to have eternal life. Likewise,
here in Luke we see that same principle, give and it
shall be given unto to you, good measure! Pressed
down! Shaken together! Running over! Sounds like
over flow to me!! Into your bosom, will men give to
you!!! Sounds, like debt cancellations, money in the
bank, unexpected checks in the mail! Listen!!! Lost
money found!! Bonuses! Raises! And Rebates!!
What I do know beloveds is the Word of God works
if you work it!

How can you apply today's devotional to your life today?

_____
_____
_____
_____
_____
_____
_____
_____
_____
_____
_____
_____
_____
_____
_____
_____
_____
_____
_____
_____
_____
_____
_____
_____
_____
_____
_____
_____

Father, thank you for being Jehovah Jireh, my
provider and source!!

DAY 8

Facing Failure

For a just man falleth seven times, and riseth up again: but the
wicked shall fall into mischief.
Rejoice not when thine enemy falleth, and let not thine heart
be glad when he stumbleth:
Lest the Lord see it, and it displease him, and he turn away
his wrath from him.
Proverbs 24:16-18

One thing is for sure beloved, that being righteous
and falling we have an assurance of when we get
back up, that God is faithful to complete the work in
us that he started. I know as one my Pastor would
say, "you need bible" Philippians 1:6 declares, the
righteous can be confident of this very thing, that
He who has begun a good work in you will
complete it until the day of Jesus Christ. There you
have it beloved, we can use that confidence to
strengthen our resolve to never give up, never to
feel like a failure or be conquered by a sense of
failure even in the event we fall seven times. On the
other hand we also see the consequences of being
wicked and it's end results as well as wisdom on
how we should respond when calamity comes upon
those who have wronged us. As disciples of Christ
Jesus, we should demonstrate his love in all things,
in all situations.

45

Now, beloved, what are your take away from today's devotion how can you apply it to your life?

_____
_____
_____
_____
_____
_____
_____
_____
_____
_____
_____
_____
_____
_____
_____
_____
_____
_____
_____
_____
_____
_____
_____

Father, thank you for helping me to
overcome my failures!!

DAY 9

Facing Fear

There is no fear in love; but perfect love casteth out fear:
because fear hath torment. He that feareth is not made perfect
in love.
1 John 4:18 (KJV)

There is no fear in love [dread does not exist]. But perfect
(complete, full-grown) love drives out fear, because fear
involves [the expectation of divine] punishment, so the one
who is afraid [of God's judgment] is not perfected in love [has
not grown into a sufficient understanding of God's love].
1 John 4:18 (AMP)

Whew, in the Greek translation perfected is teleioo
meaning maturity and completeness. We see it is
impossible to walk in the maturity and
completeness of love and fear at the same time
beloved at the same time we see the antidote for
getting rid of fear. LOVE. We see the ingredients of
fear, which is punishment we have to trust the fact
that when Jesus went to the cross beloved he took
all our stuff with him and we have no reasons to
walk in fear of judgement, we can walk securely in
the love of God.

What are your take a way's from today's devotion?

_____
_____
_____
_____
_____
_____
_____
_____
_____
_____
_____
_____
_____
_____
_____
_____
_____
_____
_____
_____
_____
_____
_____
_____
_____
_____
_____
_____

Father, thank you for allowing me to overcome my
fears with Love!!

DAY 10

Facing Finances

Therefore take no thought, saying, what shall we eat? or,
What shall we drink? or, Wherewithal shall we be clothed?
(For after all these things do the Gentiles seek:) for your
heavenly Father knoweth that ye have need of all these things.
But seek ye first the kingdom of God, and his righteousness;
and all these things shall be added unto you.
Take therefore no thought for the morrow: for the morrow
shall take thought for the things of itself. Sufficient unto the
day is the evil thereof.
Matthew 6:31-34

Jesus gives us a powerful lesson here about finances
and how we need not to worry about the cares of
life. Listen, how many times have we sang the song,
"You're a Good, Good, Father"; do we believe the
words that we sing? Do we believe and trust them?
Jesus, was giving us that assurance in this passage
of scripture. We belong to the Father, we are his
master pieces. The passages above even talk about
how the birds get fed, and the trees and lilies of the
field are also maintained, aren't we more important
than they? God knows we need food, clothes, and
shelter. He is God, he is omniscient, he knows
everything, yet Jesus gives us a principle, yes,
although he knows you need all these things you
have no need to worry about them; here is a

kingdom principle; seek ye first the kingdom of God, and his righteousness; and all, the food, the clothes, the finances, your peace, joy, that education, that job and etc....shall be added unto you and honey, you don't have to worry about tomorrow it is going to take care of itself.

Below write one thing after reading today's devotion where you will trust God with your financial needs.

_____

_____

_____

_____

_____

_____

_____

_____

_____

_____

_____

_____

_____

_____

_____

_____

_____

_____

_____

_____

_____

_____

_____

_____

_____

Father, I seek your righteousness that all
things may be added unto me!!

HELPING U
GET
STRONGER!
ISAIAH 40:29

DAY 11

Freedom

Then said Jesus to those Jews which believed on him, if ye continue in my word, then are ye my disciples indeed; And ye shall know the truth, and the truth shall make you free. They answered him, we be Abraham's seed, and were never in bondage to any man: how sayest thou, Ye shall be made free? Jesus answered them, Verily, verily, I say unto you, whosoever committeth sin is the servant of sin. And the servant abideth not in the house for ever: but the Son abideth ever. If the Son therefore shall make you free, ye shall be free indeed.
John 8:31-36

Jesus gives the antidote to freedom!!! Listen to it beloved, believe on Him, continue in His Word, which makes you a disciplined follower of Jesus, which will qualify you to know the truth, that shall make you FREE!! Somebody better catch me!! Look, I can drop pen and paper right here and close the book, but it isn't time it's only day 11. Smile. Jesus, don't be playing y'all. Now, it is a sad thing when people in bondage and don't know it, nonetheless, beloved I would like you to focus on this antidote Jesus has given today just in case there may be something going on in your life you may be struggling with, Jesus came to your house today, yes, right where you are to let you know you no longer have to be bound by that thing, yea that thing right there that just crossed your mind, that just sprung up in your belly, God wants you free today beloved and free indeed. You don't have to walk away from this moment bound. Remember whosoever committeth meaning continue in sin is the servant of sin.

Today God wants to set you free and free indeed. If you want to be free say a little prayer with me.

Let's pray

Father, I have sinned, I am asking for your forgiveness for every sin and iniquity I have committed, I confess Jesus is your son, he died and was raised from the dead for me and I believe this in my heart and your word says if I believe these truths and confess it with my mouth I am saved. Thank you Father in Jesus name for saving me! Amen!

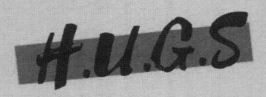

HELPING U
GET
STRONGER!
ISAIAH 40:29

DAY 12

God's Presence

Fear thou not; for I am with thee: be not dismayed; for I am thy God: I will strengthen thee; yea, I will help thee; yea, I will uphold thee with the right hand of my righteousness.
Isaiah 41:10

Here Beloveds, God graces us to know the benefits of being in his presence. The first benefit is there is no fear in the presence of God and the opposite of fear is peace (I am with you). The second benefit is we have established relationship in his presence, (I am your God). The third benefit is God's assurance of strength, help and victory over sin and death is certain. There is no better help we know than the help of the Lord himself to aid us, to strengthen us, to uphold us and protect us. I often say there is nothing like the presence of the Lord! That is the place of great exchange!!

Write an area of your life where you need to invite the presence of the Lord to invade your territory.

_____
_____
_____
_____
_____
_____
_____
_____
_____
_____
_____
_____
_____
_____
_____
_____
_____
_____
_____
_____
_____
_____
_____
_____
_____
_____
_____

Father, thank you for your Presence,
because in it is fullness of Joy!

DAY 13

God's Will

And be not conformed to this world: but be ye transformed by
the renewing of your mind, that you may prove what is that
good, and acceptable, and perfect, will of God.
Romans 12:2

Paul encourages us in the above scripture DO NOT
be conformed to this worldly system of thinking and
living because it is not the will of our Father,
instead he admonishes us to be transformed in our
English term means to change, in Greek translation
it is metamorphoo, meaning metamorphosis, which
is still change from inside out. In being transformed
we have to spend time in God's presence, in his
word meditating on it and in a place of worship. As
I stated in the previous devotion this is where the
great exchange takes place. Where our will
transforms into his will? This is where our lives
change from the how I feel or what do I do into us
actually seeing the acceptable and perfect will of
God being demonstrated in our lives.

Write down some area of your life you will work on this week to you need to be transformed in and how are you going to work on doing it.

_____
_____
_____
_____
_____
_____
_____
_____
_____
_____
_____
_____
_____
_____
_____
_____
_____
_____
_____
_____
_____
_____
_____
_____
_____

Father, thank you for allowing me to transform my mind into your perfect will.

DAY 14

Hope

I wait for the Lord, my soul doth wait, and in his word do I
hope.
Psalms 130:5

Sometimes, we find ourselves in seasons of wait
and the flesh doesn't like to wait and we get
impatient. In those times I find that the best thing to
do is to get in a quiet corner with my word, because
that is as I like to say it a very crucial time for me.
It's not a time to engage in a lot of conversation, it's
not a time to become very opinionated; you
probably say why so? I'm glad you ask. That can be
the very time you are in a season of decision
making and guess who else knows it, yes, you got it
the devil and not only does he know it your soul
does also and everything has a voice believe it or
not beloved. The psalmist makes the wisest decision
here when we are in this season of our lives, we
should turn to our word, as we wait we should
pursue the counsel of the Lord and not give room
for any other voice to invade our space. We should
definitely put all our reliance, trust and hope in the
word of the Lord.

What are your take a ways from today's devotions?

_____

_____

_____

_____

_____

_____

_____

_____

_____

_____

_____

_____

_____

_____

_____

_____

_____

_____

_____

_____

_____

_____

_____

_____

_____

Father, I wait patiently for you and my
hope is in you!

DAY 15

Humility

Let nothing be done through strife or vainglory; but in
lowliness of mind let each esteem other better than
themselves. Look not every man on his own things, but every
man also on the things of others.
Philippians 2:3-4

Paul teaches us to walk in humility, to not be selfish
and to not do things to impress people and belittle
others, but lift them up more highly than ourselves.
He also teaches us not to be just thinking of our
own success, but the success of others. This is the
picture of what true humility looks like. It is not
selfish, it is not self-ambitious, not full of vainglory
nor strife, thinking of others more highly than
themselves, and thinking of others success as well
as their own.

Can you think of a time when you demonstrated a
time of humility?

Write it here.

_____

_____

_____

_____

_____

_____

_____

_____

_____

_____

_____

_____

_____

_____

_____

_____

_____

_____

_____

_____

_____

_____

_____

Father, teach me to be humble, In Jesus Name!

HELPING U
GET
STRONGER!
ISAIAH 40:29

PART 2

H. U. G. S. (HELPING U GET STRONGER)

IN THIS PART OF THE DEVOTION WE WILL ALLOW YOU TO EXERCISE YOUR DEVOTIONAL SKILLS LET'S GO!!!

DAY 16

Integrity

He layeth up sound wisdom for the righteous: he is
a buckler to them that walk uprightly.
Proverbs 2:7

Write a prayer point from today's devotion:

_____
_____
_____
_____
_____
_____
_____
_____
_____
_____
_____
_____
_____
_____
_____
_____
_____
_____
_____

HELPING U
GET
STRONGER!
ISAIAH 40:29

DAY 17

Joy

But the fruit of the Spirit is love, joy, peace, longsuffering,
gentleness, goodness, faith, Meekness, temperance: against
such there is no law.
Galatians 5:22-23

Tell me how can you apply Joy to an area of your
life.

_____

_____

_____

_____

_____

_____

_____

_____

_____

_____

_____

_____

_____

_____

_____

Father, thank you for giving me Joy,
unspeakable Joy!

DAY 18

Love

Charity suffereth long, and is kind; charity envieth not; charity
vaunteth not itself, is not puffed up, Doth not behave itself
unseemly, seeketh not her own, is not easily provoked,
thinketh no evil; Rejoiceth not in iniquity, but rejoiceth in the
truth; Beareth all things, believeth all things, hopeth all things,
endureth all things.
1 Corinthians 13:4-7

Out of today's devotion can you write areas where
you can grow in your love language, if so write
them down and apply it this week.

_____

_____

_____

_____

_____

_____

_____

_____

_____

_____

_____

Father, thank you for an impartation of
your LOVE!

DAY 19

Mercy

Let us therefore come boldly unto the throne of grace that we
may obtain mercy, and find grace to help in time of need.
Hebrews 4:16

Today I would like to challenge you to write a
prayer point from today's devotional.

_____

_____

_____

_____

_____

_____

_____

_____

_____

_____

_____

_____

_____

_____

_____

_____

_____

_____

Father, thank you for your mercy and your grace!

H E L P I N G   U
G E T
S T R O N G E R !
I S A I A H   4 0 : 2 9

DAY 20

Marriage

The Pharisees also came unto him, tempting him, and saying unto him, Is it lawful for a man to put away his wife for every cause? And he answered and said unto them, Have ye not read, that he which made them at the beginning made them male and female, And said, For this cause shall a man leave father and mother, and shall cleave to his wife: and they twain shall be one flesh? Wherefore they are no more twain, but one flesh. What therefore God hath joined together, let not man put asunder. They say unto him, Why did Moses then command to give a writing of divorcement, and to put her away? He saith unto them, Moses because of the hardness of your hearts suffered you to put away your wives: but from the beginning it was not so.
Matthew 19:3-8

After reading todays devotional, write your take a way's.

_____
_____
_____
_____
_____
_____
_____
_____

Father, I thank you for your covenant
example of marriage!

HELPING U
GET
STRONGER!
ISAIAH 40:29

DAY 21

Obedience

And Samuel said, Hath the Lord as great delight in burnt
offerings and sacrifices, as in obeying the voice of the Lord?
Behold, to obey is better than sacrifice, and to hearken than
the fat of rams.
1 Samuel 15:22

Fill in the blank.

Behold, to _____ is better than

_____,

Do God desire sacrifices above obedience based on
today's devotional?

_____
_____
_____
_____
_____
_____
_____
_____
_____
_____
_____

Lord, I want to obey you in every area of
my life!

HELPING U
GET
STRONGER!
ISAIAH 40:29

DAY 22

Patience

And not only so, but we glory in tribulations also: knowing
that tribulation worketh patience; And patience, experience;
and experience, hope: And hope maketh not ashamed; because
the love of God is shed abroad in our hearts by the Holy Ghost
which is given unto us.
Romans 5:3-5

Write a prayer point from today's devotional.

_____
_____
_____
_____
_____
_____
_____
_____
_____
_____
_____
_____
_____
_____
_____
_____
_____

Father, I pray for the grace to be patient in
Jesus Name!

DAY 23

Peace

Be careful for nothing; but in everything by prayer and
supplication with thanksgiving let your requests be made
known unto God.
And the peace of God, which passeth all understanding, shall
keep your hearts and minds through Christ Jesus.
Philippians 4:6-7

How can you apply today's devotion to your daily life?

_____
_____
_____
_____
_____
_____
_____
_____
_____
_____
_____
_____
_____
_____
_____

DAY 24

Repentance

Cast me not away from thy presence; and take not thy holy spirit from me.

Restore unto me the joy of thy salvation; and uphold me with thy free spirit.

Then will I teach transgressors thy ways; and sinners shall be converted unto thee.

Psalms 51:11-13

What are yours take away from today devotion:

_____
_____
_____
_____
_____
_____
_____
_____
_____
_____
_____
_____
_____
_____

DAY 25

Restoration

But the God of all grace, who hath called us unto his eternal glory by Christ Jesus, after that ye have suffered a while, make you perfect, stablish, strengthen, settle you.
1 Peter 5:10

Name some of the things that are listed in today's devotion that happens after you endure suffering.

_____
_____
_____
_____
_____
_____
_____
_____
_____
_____
_____
_____
_____
_____
_____
_____

Father, thank you firmly establishing me in
the faith!

DAY 26

Self/Esteem Self/Worth

O lord, thou hast searched me, and known me. Thou knowest my downsitting and mine uprising, thou understandest my thought afar off. Thou compassest my path and my lying down, and art acquainted with all my ways. For there is not a word in my tongue, but, lo, O Lord, thou knowest it altogether. Thou hast beset me behind and before, and laid thine hand upon me. Such knowledge is too wonderful for me; it is high, I cannot attain unto it.
Psalms 139:1-6

What are some ways you can apply todays devotion to your life?

_____

_____

_____

_____

_____

_____

_____

_____

_____

_____

_____

_____

Father, I thank you that you thought I was worth saving. You know my worth.

DAY 27

Strength

Now our Lord Jesus Christ himself, and God, even our Father, which hath loved us, and hath given us everlasting consolation and good hope through grace, comfort your hearts, and stablish you in every good word and work .
2 Thessalonians 2:16-17

Write a prayer point for today's devotional.

_____

_____

_____

_____

_____

_____

_____

_____

_____

_____

_____

_____

_____

_____

_____

145

Father, give me strength for the journey!

H E L P I N G   U
G E T
S T R O N G E R !
I S A I A H   4 0 : 2 9

DAY 28

Temptation

My brethren, count it all joy when ye fall into divers
temptations; Knowing this, that the trying of your faith
worketh patience. But let patience have her perfect work, that
ye may be perfect and entire, wanting nothing. Blessed is the
man that endureth temptation: for when he is tried, he shall
receive the crown of life, which the Lord hath promised to
them that love him. Let no man say when he is tempted, I am
tempted of God: for God cannot be tempted with evil, neither
tempteth he any man:
James 1:2-4:12-13

What are your take away from today and how can you apply them to your life?

_____

_____

_____

_____

_____

_____

_____

_____

_____

_____

_____

Father, cause me to overcome ever temptation!

DAY 29

Uncertainty

Surely he shall deliver thee from the snare of the fowler, and from the noisome pestilence. He shall cover thee with his feathers, and under his wings shalt thou trust: his truth shall be thy shield and buckler. Thou shalt not be afraid for the terror by night; nor for the arrow that flieth by day; Nor for the pestilence that walketh in darkness; nor for the destruction that wasteth at noonday. A thousand shall fall at thy side, and ten thousand at thy right hand; but it shall not come nigh thee.
Psalms 91:3-7

What is a time you faced uncertainty and from today's devotion would handle differently?

_____

_____

_____

_____

_____

_____

_____

_____

_____

_____

_____

Father, I thank you that every uncertainty
is settled in you!

Work

And whatsoever ye do, do it heartily, as to the Lord, and not
unto men;
Colossians 3:23

Write a prayer from today's devotion and give one
way you can apply it to you everyday life.

_____

_____

_____

_____

_____

_____

_____

_____

_____

_____

_____

_____

_____

_____

_____

_____

_____

_____

Father, thank you for the ability to
accomplish things while working!

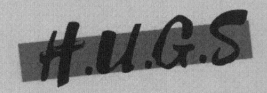

H E L P I N G   U
G E T
S T R O N G E R !
I S A I A H   4 0 : 2 9

About the Author

Sister Vickie Willis, is a god fearing woman of God
that loves people and God. She loves spending time
with her family and sharing the glorious gospel of
the Lord Jesus the Christ.

In this devotional you will be compelled to embrace
a more intimate relationship with the Lord Jesus as
Vickie walks you through daily devotion and
practical principles like no other devotional you
have ever read before. Helping you to get stronger!!
Isaiah 40:29

Made in the USA
Columbia, SC
06 February 2025

53426277R00091